A SONG FOR YOU

Women Stories in Rhyme

KAREN ELAINE O'BANNON

The only intent of these poems is to present women's experiences in an honest, thought provoking, and entertaining way that women can identify with and be inspired, encouraged, or motivated by. None of these stories are about any particular person(s) or events.

 CHICAGO SPECTRUM PRESS
4824 BROWNSBORO CENTER
LOUISVILLE, KENTUCKY 40207
502-899-1919

Printed in the U.S.A.

10 9 8 7 6 5 4 3 2 1

ISBN: 1-58374-135-6
         978-1-58374-135-1

Additional copies can be ordered from:

Karen O'Bannon
PO Box 2185
Louisville, KY 40201
www.KarenoBannon.com

To Cora Louise Franklin,
the definition of a real woman.

Acknowledgments

Thanks to everyone who kept me encouraged during the writing of this book. I especially would like to thank Cynthia Torp for helping me clarify my vision, Stremelyne Graphics for their work on my cover, and my fellow coworkers at Fed Ex Kinko's downtown for their assistance. I would also like to thank my cover girls Candice Starks, Christina Harris, Denise Dukes, LaTorri Hathaway, Caren Flewellen, and MyLeesa Mahomes. Thank you to Yvette Aghtonwest and DeVone Holt for your advice, my husband, Herbert, for allowing me the time and space to get it all done, and my Father in Heaven for giving me something to write about.

Contents

Alter Call

Women of Color

Calling all women of color.
Today is your day to arise.
Put on your banner of pride.
As you answer the call, call another.

The world is your oyster, abide.
Discover it's yours for the taking.
Our history is now in the making.
Let's walk through the door side by side.

Women declare it's your time.
Stand up and answer the call.
We must be part of it all.
Open your eyes, rise, and shine!

Knowledge Woman

All hail the woman full of knowledge.
She got straight A's and went to college.
Got that job 'cause she was polished.
Flashed her smile and they liked her style.

Entered the work force first as a desk clerk.
Moved on up 'cause she knew how to network.
She wouldn't stop 'cause the sky was her limit.
Went to the top 'cause she was in it to win it.

While she was working the haters played.
When they left work, Knowledge Woman stayed.
When the work paid off and the accolades came,
All of a sudden they had something to say.

Some questioned what her rise was really about.
Some tried to take advantage of her new clout.
Some had outrageous criticisms to spout.
Some were manipulative and wanted her out.

But don't hate 'cause Knowledge Woman
Knew what she wanted,
Had a dream, set a goal, took a chance, and got on it.
Don't hate 'cause she's living her life like its golden.
Tell the truth, you weren't ready
And that's why you weren't chosen.

Get your own dreams, make plans,
And get in the race.
Feel the force, stay the course,
And find your own place.

I Believe

I believe in the oneness
Of mind, body, and soul.
I believe all three should be healthy
In order for one to be whole.

I believe in the circle of life.
I believe the body is a temple.
I believe peace conquers strife.
I believe in keeping things simple.

I believe there's a beginning,
Middle, and ending to everything.
I believe that persistence gives
Life to a dream.

I believe that possibilities can be found
In just about anything.
I believe that two are better than one.
I believe a group works best as a team.

I believe a person's word
Should be a person's bond.
I believe by-gone
Should really be by-gone.

I believe a good story
Deserves to be told.
I believe it's never too late,
Nor are you ever too old.
I believe in helping others.
I believe children should be given wings,
Not smothered.

I believe that everyone deserves a chance.
I believe in love that leads to romance.
I believe that in marriage
Two really become one.

I believe Jesus is God's only begotten Son.
I believe that dreams can and do come true.
I believe in myself, of course.
And I believe in you.

Schedule

Work hard, play hard
Is what I say.
I work my job
Like a Hebrew slave.
When Friday comes
I dance the night away.
Household chores
On Saturday.
Sunday morning
I give Him praise.

Advice

Strength starts with courage.
Let your life flourish.
Keep your dreams nourished.

Choose the right mate.
Let him ask for your hand.
Respect you must demand.

Don't forget to pray.
The Lord makes a way.
You have what you say.

Learn as you live.
Try to forgive.
Focus on the positive.

I Choose

There will always be dream busters
Standing in the way
Wishing bad things on you,
Trying to block everything you do.
Those negative, doubting adversaries
Who hate you because you're not ordinary.

But I won't be defined
By their perception, you see.
What constitutes victory
Has already been decided by me.
I choose to take advantage of every possibility,
To disregard their negativity,
To keep company with those like me.

Whether I win or lose,
My life will be lived by the goals I choose.
My dreams are my reality.
I'm the one I'll try to please.
If God be for me, I can't lose.
So the path I take, I'll choose.

Dream Team

There once was a girl named Erica Strong
Who lived in a place where she didn't belong.
But she held on tight to a very big dream
That she hid in her heart because she truly believed.

Even though she knew others dreamed dreams, too.
They had tried like her, but they couldn't break
through.
Yes, she knew that the road would be long.
So she prayed for the strength to stay strong.
She lived for the day to prove nay Sayers wrong.
A plan she began to execute.

But, as Erica launched her attack,
She realized there were things that she lacked.
Something was amiss.
She couldn't make the pieces fit.
Then just in the knick of time,
A mentor was sent to assist.

The mentor strengthened her in the areas where she
lacked,
Taught her the professional way to act,
Hooked her up with legitimate contacts, and
Put her on the right road.
That gave her the confidence to be bold.
And guess what?
Her idea sold.

Then right before her eyes
Her dream materialized.

Love Me Knots

Like A River

Like a river, still.
Emotions hide,
Buried deep inside, and
Driven by enlightened pride
Caused by foolish days gone by.
They won't come alive.
She doesn't think they can
For him or any other man.
It's not in the plan.
But, then again. . .

Like a river, deep.
Love keeps right on calling.
Her heart knows what's at stake.
It can no longer shake
Its desperate need to undertake.
But love is far below the surface.
Will it fulfill its purpose?
Is this the beginning or the end?
Can love live again?

Love Triangle

It was getting dark.
The night was growing old.
A triangle of love was about to unfold.
Boyfriend came into the house
Feeling down and out.
Girlfriend tried to consol him,
But he straight shut her out.

Girlfriend knew she had to handle him gently.
Boyfriend started getting uptight,
Brushing off every act of her kindness,
Claiming that he was alright.
But what Boyfriend was really doing
Was trying to pick a fight.
He was trying to get to Man Stealer's house
With an excuse to spend the night.

Meanwhile, Girlfriend was trying not to fight.
But it was crystal clear to her
That something wasn't right.
So, she questioned him.
He started lying.
They started hollering.
She started crying.
Then, right on cue, he left
And she knew.

Now home alone
And wondering what to do,
Girlfriend decided
Not to sit there and stew.
She got on the phone,
Called Man Stealer a so and so,

Made her intentions clear,
And clicked the phone in her ear.

Man Stealer called her right back.
Gave her some retaliation flack.
She said she didn't appreciate
Being called out of her name.
Told her not to hate the player,
But to hate the game.
She said she wasn't going down without a fight.
And if Girlfriend didn't like it,
It could be on tonight.

During all this time
Do you know what boyfriend was doing?
Instead of offering intervention,
He was enjoying the attention.
See, he was flattered
To have two ladies fighting over him.
And he had already decided
He'd be with whoever wins.

Anyway, Man Stealer is fired up now.
She decides to turn the night
Into a final showdown.
So an hour later
She's knocking on Girlfriend's door
Yelling for her to come outside
If she thinks she wants some more.

What did she do that for?
Girlfriend wasn't about
To let that slide.
Before Man Stealer
Could finish her sentence
Girlfriend had stepped outside.

The next thing you know
A screaming match had ensued.
And the whole neighborhood
Came out to watch the two fools.
They were laughing and pointing
At them both from afar.
While Boyfriend watched the whole thing
From inside of his car.

Girlfriend went into a ranting rage.
Then Man Stealer hollered her piece.
After that went on for a while
Someone finally called the police.
Once the police came
And somewhat resolved it,
Now here comes Boyfriend
Wanting to get involved in it.

He wants to profess his love
And apologize to Girlfriend.
Of course, you and I know
He only did that
'Cause he wanted to get back in.
He told Man Stealer
She needed to go home
Now that he and Girlfriend were on the mend.
He hoped that she wouldn't be too upset.
After all, they were only friends.

So things settled down and got quiet.
Girlfriend and Boyfriend
Were about to turn in.
When all of a sudden
Ring, ring went the phone.
And it started all over again.

Love Loss

This is a story about Eve and her man.
She loved him very much, but didn't understand
What she needed to do to complete him.
She would have to fight hard just to keep him.
But, in the end, she wouldn't win
Because it wasn't meant to be.

You see, before they met he and she both had
Different ways of doing things.
And, although they both knew it,
They thought power was in their rings.
Then along came a spider baring peace the man desired.
Because he was sick and tired, he let the spider in.
And, you guessed it, a very steamy romance began.

When the news got back to Eve,
She demanded to know
Every detail from start to finish of the entire episode.
He didn't want to do it
Because he knew she would explode, and rightly so;
But he did, just trying to be honest,
And boy did Eve unload.

It was looking pretty grim for the two of them.
And then it got quiet. All the yelling came to an end.
Now I know you think you know what happened,
But I'm telling you you'd be wrong.
The man loved Eve. He didn't leave her.
She didn't put him out either,
Despite the fact that together they were wrong.

He renewed his vows of love and protection.
Eve got all that he had (well, almost).
What she clearly lacked was his warmth and affection.

He had given that away, and couldn't get it back.
It was the spider he craved.

Eve had won the battle, not the war.
The burden became an awful chore.
She often dreamed of something more.
And, occasionally, when things got rough,
When it seemed like things were just too tough,
She entertained thoughts of divorcing him,
But stayed until the end.

More Than is Not Enough

She was more than a notion,
More than a fling.
It was more than puppy love
Or a friendship ring.

But it wasn't enough to get love in motion.
It was certainly not a forever thing.
The idea of marriage wasn't given a thought,
And definitely no offspring.

Even though she was clearly adored.
Good times deserved an encore.
Yet, despite her obvious charm,
Or the way he felt in her arms,
Simply put, she wasn't the one.

The person she was couldn't change it
Be it the short or long range of it.
This was a fact Mr. Man understood.
And to him everything was all good.

Not telling her made good sense
If he could just keep up the pretense.
So not a word would he say to her.
His lips would be sealed until he met the real girl.

Vacation

On our beach towels the two of us
Laugh with the sea.
Blue skies are above us,
My man and me.

We're sampling the water,
Catching the breeze,
And nibbling on fruit
That we picked from the trees.

There's really no hurry.
We have no worries.
I'm with my man,
And my man is with me.

Inter-Racial Lover

Inter-racial lover, milky valentine,
Smooth with extra butter
Who's chosen to be mine.
I'm talking about my man.
Holler if you understand.

I've dated lots of brothers.
There was nothing wrong with them.
I just didn't have the chemistry
I seem to have with him.

My inter-racial man
Sees the world much differently.
There are no ties that bind us,
No walls,
No glass ceiling.
I find it quite appealing
To have no limits on my dreams.

I'm superwoman.
Can't do wrong.
He's proud of my blackness.
Together we're strong.
I'm persuaded I belong.

And I can't help it.
All my fears have melted
In the arms of my non-black lover.
I believe now that I've felt it.

Mr. Popular

There he was, Mr. Popular,
A fine specimen of a man.
He was a teenage heart throb.
He was also a gentleman.

His neck and wrist always
Sprinkled with a subtle bling.
He was dressed to the nine
All the time. Stayed clean.

He was a great conversationalist,
Had a big white smile,
And he drove a Miata
Top down, my style.

The problem was
That the boy liked to play around.
Regardless of what type of girl,
He knew how to lay it down.

I had a crush on him,
And he was flirting with me.
Being his girlfriend
Was my high school fantasy.
But in reality I knew
I was just another pretty face to pursue.

It was never going to be him and me, you see.
There were too many girls chasing him,
Not enough boys chasing me.
So I vowed not to be
The one hanging on a string.
Play the fool? Not cool.
That would never be me.

But when the moment arrived,
I was hypnotized.
He was holding me tight
And stealing kisses left and right.

My eyes were open, but I was blind.
I was leaving my plans behind.
That boy had me feeling all right.
Had me wondering what the rest of him was like.

His words kept calling, calling, calling.
I felt myself falling, falling, falling.
He was singing his song. I was humming along,
And at the same time trying to fight.
But resisting would take all of my might.

I had to concentrate.
It was about to be too late.
Uneasiness was on the increase.
I didn't want to lose my peace.

I needed to break free from his thrust.
I needed to put distance between us.
I was out on a limb.
I had to get away from him.

So I did it.
I made up my mind to quit.
And, when he was nowhere around,
I climbed down.

My Truth

It was an exciting time.
I was only twenty-five
When Johnny came into my life.
He was thirty and kind of flirty.
We hit it off right away
And, before long, I became his wife.

We wore rings, had a nice home,
Nice cars, nice clothes, and everything.
But, after a while, I began to feel
Like something else was still missing.

I went to church every Sunday,
As I had done since I was a youth.
But one particular day
I heard the message in a new way,
And it became my Truth.

I mean it changed me.
And for the next five years
I waited for Johnny's soul to change.
He wasn't ready though,
And found my behavior to be strange.

I lost my interest in the club life,
My drinking habits began to wane,
And I could make a conversation
About Jesus out of a
Conversation about anything.
We had love,
But we'd lost that in love
Kind of feeling.
I knew without a miracle

We wouldn't make it,
And that would kill me.

I prayed
For God to strengthen all our doubts.
But Johnny didn't want strength.
He just wanted out.

So, here we are,
Two people once in love
Going separate ways.
But I still have my Truth,
And it's going to be okay.

The Apology

"I'm sorry," he said.
"Please accept my confession.
I was out of control.
What I did wasn't cool,
And I've learned my lesson.
My intention was never to hurt you.

I just wasn't thinking, you see.
Well, I was, just not about you.
At the time it was all about me.
And I completely and deeply apologize
For all of your pain and grief."

He assured me that regardless of what he had done,
In the matter of love, I was the one.
He repeated that softly again in my ear.
He kissed away every one of my tears,
Looked deep into my eyes,
And, again, apologized.

"That's why I want to work through it," he said.
"I know if we try we can do it," he pled.
"Have a scream and shout fest.
Get it all off your chest.
Whatever it takes I'll do for our sake."
And he left me with a decision to make.
But this is too big to work out alone.
I don't make good choices too well on my own.
I've prayed, I've cried, and I still can't decide.
All I know is that I want to come out with my pride
Intact.

The fact is that
It hurts to think of life without him
Because I care so much about him.

But I can't go through this pain anymore.
I really need to close this door.

That's why I called you.
Will you walk me through?
If I need to, can I call and talk to you?
Will you make sure that I do it?
Will you stay until the end?
Will you wipe my tears until I mend?

Even If

It's over.
But I don't want to
Cry about it.
Even if I wanted to
Cry about it I couldn't
Because I've cried
Over you before.
So I'm not going to.

Even if I did cry
You'd never know
Because, if you knew,
You might realize
How much I love you.

But, even if you knew
How much I love you,
You'd be wrong to
Get the idea that
I'd miss you enough
To take you back.
 I wouldn't.

Even if I could.

The Friend Zone

The Message

Hey, Girl! What's up?
I was thinking about you today.
I was wondering what you've been up to,
And if everything is okay.

I was thinking about what a good friend
You've been and are to me.
Thinking about how long it's been
Since we last shot the breeze.
Thinking about not letting our friendship
Slip into the past.
Thinking about how I said I would call
The very next time I got a chance.

I was hoping that we could get
Together again real soon.
Hoping that we could catch up on
Each other's latest news.
Hoping that we could maybe even
Hang out for a little while.
Hoping that we could reminisce together
Old school style.

Just wanted to tell you that all is well
And I am doing fine.
I hope you get this message.
Call me back when you have some time.

Lonely Woman

Lonely Woman, lonely as can be.
You love my man, but my man's with me.
That's what you get for trying to be a thief.
Now you must pay with the pain of your grief.

When he and I met it was kind of like magic.
I was very talkative. He was very shy.
In the areas he was weak, I was strong.
We thrived.
We were a couple on a mission,
Stood together unified,
And we trusted one another
Until death with our lives.

Then it seemed like our good thing
Might be coming to an end.
We hit a fork in the road, and,
For a while, were barely friends.
And just when we were about
To get things back together again,
Here you come with your sneaky self
Trying to get my man.

You came into it
Trying to act so concerned.
But what you were really doing
Was trying to see what you could learn.
You even called me friend.
But, as soon as my back was turned,
You made your move, and I got burned.
Okay, so he was with you.
But his loyalty to me didn't turn.

Did you really think that you
Would get away with your sin?

Did you believe for one moment
That you had a chance to win?
Trying to force an ultimatum
Is what became the death of you.
He didn't leave. Now you're through.
Good for me. Bad for you.

But what's saddest about the whole thing
Is that it never had to be.
If you'd just left us alone
We would have worked it out eventually.
But, since you tried to take
Someone who wasn't available to you,
All kinds of unnecessary issues have ensued.
But don't worry about it. I'm staying.
We'll work through all that, too,
Because I'd rather straighten out this mess
Than give my man to you.

End of a Friend

I've said it before and I'd say it again. . .
I'm not your enemy. I'm your friend.
I would never do anything to intentionally hurt you.
That's not who I am.
That's not the kind of thing I do.
Your ultimate good is what I desire.
It's me who encourages you to aspire.
I'd say it, that is, if I were talking to you.
But I'm not.
Our friendship is over because I'm through.

I gave you a truth like a real friend would.
Unfortunately, you misunderstood.
If you had questions about what I said,
Why couldn't you just come to me
And give me the opportunity
To help you clear your head?
Instead, you chose to speak your mind
To people who don't know and weren't there.
I don't know why you thought they'd even care.
But it seems to me like you'd rather be deceived
By them than be a friend to me.

What's that about?
No matter what we've been through,
One thing should stand out.
I've been in your corner since we were little kids.
What more is there to prove?
Have I ever made a major move without consulting you?
So, after everything we've been through,
How could you be so crude?

By the way, this is not the first time
Your mind took a trip that made you flip
And caused your tongue to slip,

After which you act like nothing's wrong,
And I play along because I know that's how you are.
But this dance has gone on too long.
In fact, this time you went too far.

If I were talking to you, I'd want you to explain
Because I'm confused.
I'm sure it keeps you entertained,
But I am not amused.
And I refuse to go through it anymore.
It's no way to treat a friend.
See yourself to the door.

Love Jones

The girl is in love.
I mean she's all the way in.
It's mad, crazy love
That she plans to stay in.

Whatever I would tell her about him
She would not believe.
Instead, all the blame that belongs to him
Would be transferred onto me.

So I'm not saying a doggone thing.
I just want to make it clear
That whichever way the chips fall
My support will be right here.

Just Friends

I love you with the love of God,
But I am not in love with you.
Get that straight, Flirty One.
I am not your mate.

You've told everyone you know
That God has given me to you.
But I wasn't given a clue.
According to me, it's not true.

And I'm not saying
That God said or didn't say anything.
All I'm saying is whatever He said to you
He hasn't said to me.

So, could you please
Keep our supposed future to yourself
Or let it be
Until God speaks to both you and me?

Gossiper

Do you know the kind of person who's
Always trying to get the latest news
On anybody about anything
Whether or not any of it is true?
I do. It's you.

Whenever gossip is going down
I can bet my paycheck you'll be around
Trying to get the latest low down
So that you can be the first to spread it around.
Oh, yes. It's true.

But your gossipy ways are getting old.
And it's time someone finally told you so.
You're not a true friend, and it's starting to show.
You hear a rumor, and your lips start to go.
Oh, yes. They do.

A person is known by the seeds that she sows.
Gossip is not how I want to be known.
The only one's business to share is your own.
Stop all of your talking, or leave me alone.
It's up to you.

Just Serious

In Her Mind

There's an old woman in my neighborhood
Who doesn't put herself together quite right.
She wears too much make-up.
It's thick.
Too much blush,
Too much lipstick,
Too many colors on her eyes.
The fact that people think she's crazy
Is no big surprise.

She wears loud and busy patterns
That compete with her perfume
Which lights the air as she passes by.
And, yet, she still has that look in her eyes.
Time has dulled her senses,
But it hasn't squashed her pride.

She's a diva,
And she was excellent in her time.
Before the weight gain,
Before the eye strain,
She was how beauty was defined.
She still remembers
And, in her mind, still owns the time.

Mad Girl

Mad Girl, Mad Girl
Why are you so sad?
Did somebody treat you bad,
Steal a dream that you once had,
Have a request of yours forbade,
Or are you going through a fad?

Mad Girl, Mad Girl
Why are you so mean?
Do you always make a scene
Every time you disagree?
If I just let you scream,
Would that set your mind at ease?

Mad Girl, Mad Girl
Always lashing out,
Flashing ugly pouts,
Making waves, no doubt
You're defeated by your mouth.

Mad Girl, Mad Girl
Educated fool,
Stubborn as a mule,
Trying to play it cool,
You're really mad at you.

Baby Girl

This story begins with Earl, an unhappy man
Who hated his life, so away he ran.
On his way to wherever he met Pearl,
Fell in love with her, and had a baby girl.
But his life didn't blow up, and when things got too tough,
He got in his car and raised the heck up.

But this story is not about him or any of that.
It's about the baby girl
Who wrote him that he never wrote back.
It's about her low self-esteem and how it begun.
It's about her trying to find her daddy's love in any someone.

The first man she met was really sweet at first, like Earl.
We'll call him Terry.
In fact, he swept her off her feet.
But, once in a while, he had to have a drink.
And when he drank too much he became her enemy.
But, since no other man had loved her,
She thought she couldn't leave.

When she announced she was going to have a baby,
Terry went out of his mind. He was already crazy.
And, instead of trying to find a way to manage them and himself,
His crazy ass flipped the script, cussed her out, and left
Just like Earl.

And now Baby Girl, who already had some issues,
Was left alone with a child of her own and a box of
Kleenex tissues.

You would have thought that everything lost
Would have taught her a valuable lesson.
It didn't.
Again and again to every loser she was drawn.

All the while Baby Girl's baby girl was growing up.
And the life her mother was living was making it hard
for her to triumph.
She hated positive women and claimed *they* had the
attitude.
But that was because she *liked* who she was.
And so the cycle continued.

Son

Now that you are almost grown
I recognize your need to own
Your space,
To find your own place.
But, on the other hand,
You are not yet a man.
And there are still things you need to know
Before I let you go,
Although
I'm sure you don't think so.

That's why I pray
Each day
That you will be okay,
That God will use whatever way He needs to
In order to get you through
As you go your own way.
And someday
I hope you will see
That all I ever wanted for you
Is all that you can be.

Random Act of Discipline

I was at an amusement park
Watching my kids on a water ride
When I spied with my little eyes
A smart-aleck young guy.

A lifeguard asked him rather nicely twice
To cross from where he was to the other side.
And he, wanting to be rude, yelled, "I heard you!,"
But didn't bother to move.

So I signaled for him to come to me.
He shot me a *You ain't talkin' to me* look,
Which I thought was whack.
I shot him a *Yes, I am,*
And you'd better get over here look right back.

I said, "I know I'm not your mother,
Just so we keep this conversation on track,
But I'm black and you're black.
Let's base our conversation on that.

The lifeguard was just doing her job.
All you had to do was move.
But, instead, and for no particular reason,
You chose to be rude.
You didn't look good doing it,
I doubt your Mama would be proud of that,
And in the eyes of some
You may have even set our people back.

Get yourself together," I said.
"Try to be more respectful," I pled.
That was my random act of discipline.
I hope the message sank in.

System Failure

Darnell is my girlfriend Doresha's son
Who went to kindergarten
And heard from someone
That parents weren't allowed to spank anymore.
To do so would bring
The police to the door.

So one night he decided to test this theory.
When bedtime came, although he was weary,
He wouldn't go to sleep.
Said he needed something to drink.
Doresha knew he'd wet the bed though.
So, in response to his question, she said, "No."
An hour later he still wouldn't go.

He asked again and again for a drink.
Doresha flatly refused.
Darnell thought that getting her mad was exciting.
Doresha was not amused.
In fact, she was getting very upset.
But Darnell wasn't giving up yet.
He decided to change his request.
"Can I go to the bathroom?" he pressed.
"Yes."

But when he stayed in the bathroom too long,
Doresha knew something was wrong.
So she peeped through the keyhole,
And caught Darnell lapping water
From the toilet bowl!
You heard me.
Then, before he could look up,
Doresha had snuck up,
Grabbed him by the arm,
And spanked his butt.

Darnell cried until his voice was hoarse.
While he cried, he questioned his source.
"I'm sorry, Mama," he eventually said.
Then, finally, he went to bed.
But Little Darnell was just a pretender.
In his mind he had not yet surrendered.
He laid there in remembrance of
The spanking he got.
He would use that pain
To get the sympathy he sought.

So, the next day when he went to school
He sulked until the teacher asked,
"Why are you blue?"
"My Mama whooped me for trying to get a drink,"
Darnell said just as he had rehearsed.
The teacher was shocked by what Darnell had said
And responded by getting the nurse.

Well, Darnell got the sympathy he wanted,
Proved the theory worked,
Outsmarted his Mama.
In fact, he had outsmarted the whole school.
The mystery was resolved.
He had managed to get the police
And child services involved.

Never mind that he lied
And his mother was blamed.
Never mind that he'd ruined
Her name and brought shame,
Or the court cost ensued,
Or that he was moved.
He didn't care.
It wasn't his burden to bear, yet.

All because he wanted to have his own way.
All because someone taught him how to run game.

All because the teacher drew a hasty conclusion.
All because he preferred the confusion.
All because Doresha tried to do what was right for
Darnell.
A home was destroyed.
The system failed.

Monkey's Uncle

I've had enough of your
Shoulda, woulda, coulda mess.
It's time to move on now.
Let's deal with the rest.

I'm sure there are many things
That, as a mother, I could have done better.
I'm equally sure the odds of our success would have increased
Had the two of us been working together.

But you weren't trying
To play the father role then.
You were either glued to the television,
Or out in the streets with your friends.

Now that she's in trouble you want to chastise her,
And you want me to back you.
But may I ask where you were
When she was doing what all this was leading up to?

I'm not arguing the point that she needs to be dealt with
Before she gets too far down the wrong path.
I'm just saying that what a monkey sees, a monkey will do.
You do the math.

What you need to do is check yourself,
While you're trying to front.
Try talking to her before you start the witch hunt.
Realize we, the parents, are partly responsible.
Then maybe we can all get what we want.

Whack Attack

"What's up, Shorty?," yelled a voice in the crowd,
An abrupt kind of voice, obnoxious and loud.
I was curious, so I looked up to see who was talking.
My eyes landed on a buster straight up gawking
At me,
Flashing yellow-stained teeth and picking up speed.

Oh, no he's not trying to holler at me
Is what I said in my mind
While looking for a way to escape his tired behind.
Why me?
But before I could find a way out of the place,
There Brother-Man was with his grill in my face.

"What's your name, Baby Girl?," he asked.
I took an involuntary step back.
Thought of offering him a comb and a tic-tac.
I didn't want to embarrass him, though.
So I held my breath for a minute or so.

I just wanted to avoid the fowl air.
Anyway, he didn't seem to care.
So what if I verged on a faint attack.
He had my attention and went on with his mack.

So there I was pretending to listen,
But in my mind praying for divine intervention.
I said, *Lord, I know I've been saying*
That my life has been dull,
That I need a man to get me out of this lull.
I even said I'd let you choose the man for me.
But this isn't what I had in mind,
Not that he has to be knock down fine,
But not this!

And I do realize it's not for me to insist,
But with this man I can't be seen.
I'm your daughter. I'm a queen! Okay a princess.
I've heard you had a sense of humor, but him. . .with me?
Could you get your laugh on
And say this brother's not the one?
Oh, and could you let someone I know walk by
Or call me on my cell phone?

I wish I could have told the brother why I wasn't
interested;
But, if I did, I'd be a so and so. Then I'd be offended.
So, I just walked away.
And that's how the conversation ended.

Space

The other day I overheard you talking
To some girl about this dude.
I was bothered by what you were saying,
As well as your attitude.

You said something about him being a no class man
And not having enough cash to spend on you.
Said his house didn't have nice furniture in it,
And you dogged his hooptie, too.

And, even though he told you
He was working full time and going to school,
You claim he's lame because
He doesn't spend all his free time with you.

It's true there are some brothers around
Whose ways are fly by night,
But should you put a man down
When his intensions appear to be right?

Give the man some space to build his dreams.
Don't be in a hurry. Step back.
Let the man get his life on track,
And you'll find that in the crop he's the cream.

Explanation, Please

Black Man, Black Man
Is there any doubt
That the womb made room for you
To make your exit out?

Then how in the world could you be so inclined
To degrade me or any sister of mine?
Tell me why because I really want to know.
From exactly what garden do your hate seeds grow?

Is it a hip thing to say?
Is it the ghetto way?
Is it your black experience?
Or is it just plain ignorance?

Does it feel good when you're calling me a hoe?
Tell me.
I just want to understand you, Bro.
Think about it, holler back, and let me know.

To My Super-Sized Sisters

I'm proud of my big sisters
For finally taking a stand,
For tearing down the wall of weight prejudice,
For having the guts to demand/to be
Free
From the stigmas that separated you
From the social kindnesses
Once only extended to the petite like me.
I think it's pretty neat
That the ping alum seems to be swinging
The other way.
There's too much emphasis
On being thin these days.

But

Despite the fact that meatier women
Are currently preferred,
Don't get it twisted, my sister,
Being proportionately curved, not bigness,
Gets the highest level of attention,
Or haven't you heard?
So don't let this be your opportunity
To flip the insult script on the sisters in the small category.
Just as some of you can't help being big,
Some sisters can't help being lien.

The tabloids may be skinny bashing right now,
But don't think they've forgotten about you.
Don't take part in their insults.
The saying what goes around comes around is true.
The fact is that the woman who holds

Her head up has nothing, and I mean nothing, to
prove.
Don't forget what it feels like
When people are being rude.

In This House

If these walls could talk
They would surely bend your ears
Telling you about stories of the life I had
Growing up here.

About being the last one at the kitchen table
Stirring my food around.
About sneaking in the house after curfew
Trying not to make a sound.

About me changing outfits in the mirror,
Going for the popular look.
About the time I burnt the Sunday dinner
Learning how to cook.

About the first time that time of the month came
And Mama and I had to have "the talk".
About the dance lessons I gave my little sister
On how to Scorpio and Moon Walk.

About card games and loud talking
With the family every Friday night.
About quiet moments on the front porch
Under a cool, starry night.

About being on the phone at night
When I was supposed to be in bed.
About rolling my eyes while my Mama fussed,
Mocking every word she said.

About the time my boyfriend came to visit
And my Dad asked a million questions.
About secrets shared with my closest friends
About truth or dare confessions.

But tonight this house is empty.
The end of this era is drawn.
I'm taking the memories with me.
Our family is moving on.

Personal Problems

The Decision

How did I get myself
Into this mess?
It's quite a situation,
I must confess.
Now your fate is
In my hands, Jane Doe.
Should I bring you in the world,
Or let you go?

I shouldn't have fallen
For his games and deceit.
I should have trusted more
In my own instincts.
I should have listened harder
To that voice inside.
I should have been much stronger
And defended my pride.

I should have thought through it
Before deciding to do it.
But I didn't.
And now I must decide
If I will spare your life or end it.

Shopping Spree Sting

It was the end of the workweek.
I had worked very hard.
A reward was due me
Through a purchase on my card.

But a voice loud and clear
Whispered something in my ear.
It said in my head,
You should stay at home instead.
Think I listened? Yeah, right.
I'll be back sometime tonight.

So, I headed to the mall
Intent on buying something small.
No sooner than I stepped inside,
I mean I was barely through the door,
My eyes found the prize
In the window of a shoe store.

I couldn't speak.
My feet wouldn't move.
I was glued to the window
Filled with cold-blooded shoes.
It was settled right then.
I had to go in.
I sat in the chair
And tried on every pair.

After about an hour in there
I made my choice, bought two pair.
My feet rejoiced.
And that was the moment I knew
I had much more shopping to do.

Off I went to another store.
That's right! I needed a matching out-fit.
The voice in my head said, *You know you need to quit!*
And I was abruptly reminded
That I was only going to buy one thing, one thing!
But the shoes had me blinded.

So I marched on, no looking back.
I viciously attacked the clothes rack,
Made sure everything fit me,
And left the store with the clothes on my back.

At home I put my make-up on.
Then I did another mirror check.
I wanted to get the full effect.
I felt myself slipping into buyer's remorse.
It was brought on by the voice in my head, of course.

What are you doing?, the voice said to me.
"I'm looking at myself!," I said. "Can't you see?
In fact, I look too good to sit up in this house.
I'm going to call my girls to see if they want to go out."
They did.
And off to the club we slid.

But the next day after I added up all I'd spent,
My so-called reward began to feel like a punishment.
Aside from the shoes and clothes
I don't even know where my money went.

Once again I heard the voice.
It said, *This whole thing was all your choice.*
I tried to stop you plenty of times,
But you wouldn't stop until you'd spent every dime.
Next time listen to me. Do something free.
Stay at home, pop some popcorn, watch TV,
And avoid the pain of a shopping spree.

Weight Obsession

Let's see.
Where do I begin?
I've got my health, my family,
My church, and my friends.

I have a good life,
But I'm unhappy right now
Because
The size I've become isn't the size that I was.

I'm not pleased with my current image.
To me it's not okay.
Others may be able to accept it,
But I'm not who my body betrays.

I'll admit I went a little crazy,
I ate too much, got a little lazy.
Now I want to go back in time.
I want to reclaim what's mine.

I want to go back to being a size 9,
5'7", 145 pounds, a C cup, and a round behind.
I want to be that woman again.
I want to be me when I was thin.

You're probably thinking it's shallow of me
To let my weight cause this misery.
But that's okay. I know what I want.
Just don't try to squash my dream.

I know that it's possible.
It's who I used to be.
And I want it enough
To back the talk up.

My mind's made up.
A thin me is who I see.

So, if you can't be encouraging,
Then just don't say anything.
And when I reach my goal
You'll stop trying to understand.
You'll know.

You're going to like what you see.
Then again, maybe you won't.
Heads are going to turn.
All eyes will be on me.

Then Me

I saw myself today
In a girl no older than ten.
My mind set the stage
To the time when
"Then Me" was around that age.

"Then Me" was a shy girl
Who desperately wanted friends in her world,
But didn't know how to conversate,
Was too shy to initiate,
And had a hard time holding on to them.

She gave away all of her favorite toys.
Even gave away her lunch at school.
She went along just to get along then
Trying to be one of the cool.

It turns out she played the fool.
It took her a while to know it.
However, she finally found the right groove.
And once she fell into it,
The quality of her friends improved.

The girl around ten
Reminded me of all that today.
I saw myself in the way she played.
She'll be on my mind for the next few days.
I hope she finds her way.

When I'm Gone

When I'm gone will anyone know I was here?
Will anyone even care?
There's nothing special about my life.
Thank goodness you were there.

You know every significant moment.
You've shared all of my pain and glory.
Will you do one thing, if you're still here when I leave?
Remember and tell my story.

Snail Pace Morning Race

I was dogged tired
When the alarm went off.
Getting ready for work is rough.
After I'd hit the snooze bar
For the fourth time,
I knew I had to get up.

So I tried to get into the groove.
I made my way to the bathroom
And sat on the toilet stool.
I got real comfortable there.
It took me a while to move.

Ten minutes later
I decided to brush my teeth.
I took a shower,
Got dressed,
And tried to find something to eat.

But I had to put a hold on food
Because one look at the clock and I knew
Time was up,
So out the door I flew.

I drag raced through the neighborhood
In an attempt not to be late,
Which we all know would not be good.
I ran inside as I've done all week,
Punched the clock in the nick of time,
And breathed a sigh of relief.

My Hair

I've got a love/hate relationship
With a particular body part.
It's my hair,
And I love/hate it with all of my heart.
I know that I am wonderfully
And marvelously made.
Nevertheless, that part of me
I would still willingly trade.
I wish it didn't bother me.
I wish I didn't care;
But I love/hate having
Nappy, high maintenance hair.

What I love about it are all of the ways
I can style it.
I can make it do things
Other hair types can't do.
I love natural styles a lot, like
Afros, pom-poms, dread locks, and knots.
I can jump into one of those hairstyles
And drop-it-like-it's-hot.
And when I feel like blending in
With the rest of the world,
I just put a perm in my hair
And hello, it's diva girl.

But there are good days and bad days.
That's where the love/hate part begins
Because it's more than a notion
To bring African Goddess or Diva Girl in.
See, my hair is complicated.
It takes time to work a style.
When I get started on it
I know I'm going to be working with it
For a while.

I tried to do it myself,
But, due to my ignorance, had to stop.
Now I spend all day once a week
In the gossip house, I mean beauty shop.
It cost me anywhere between
$25-$150 a pop.
And, once I've spent that money,
Do you think there's a happy ending?
There isn't.
I look good at that moment,
But new problems are beginning.
Now my hair becomes the diva.
She puts her demands on me.
Absolutely no forms of water must touch her, and
That's the way it has to be.

So, I can't swim without worrying
About getting my hair wet.
I can't play sports
On the chance I might sweat.
I can't wash my hair
And let it dry on its own.
I can't take a shower
Without a shower cap on.

And my man won't be running
His fingers through my hair because
It takes too much effort
Getting it back like it was.
I can't lay on it without
Wearing a scarf.
Some nights I sleep on my chin,
And you know that's crazy.
Do you see what I mean?
Where does the madness end?

It's a pain, a chore, an outright war.
To say it is not a sin,

And has nothing to do with the skin I'm in.
So, yes, I love/hate my hair.
I said it and I meant it. So there.

The Call

In the middle of the night
The phone rang
And caught me by surprise.
It was my mother
Baring the bad news
That my father had just died.

He had been ill for a while
So I shouldn't have been surprised.
But I was.
And, without notice,
Tears began to fill my eyes.

Why?
It wasn't like I was Daddy's little girl.
We didn't hang out that much.
We didn't regularly keep in touch.

Still, I was his child.
We were from the same linage.
We shared the same heritage.
It bothered me for a while.

I was sad to hear
That Daddy had passed away.
I even prayed for his soul that day.
I hoped that he was saved.

Because he believed in God
And went to church,
I choose to believe
He was.
That will have to be
Enough for me.

I'm Sorry

I'm sorry for what I did,
And when I did it,
And how I did it,
And why I did it.
I apologize.

It was not my intent to hurt you,
Or to embarrass you,
Or to front on you,
Or to desert you.
This truly is no lie.

So let me make it up to you,
Say something to you,
Do something for you
To dry your teary eyes.

I'm sorry for what I did.
The point I was making
Was clear at the time,
But I'm not so sure it was wise.
I apologize.

Nothing justifies hurting a friend.
I apologize again.

Tired

I'm tired. So you know what?
I'm deciding right now
That for the rest of the day
I'm not going to do a darn thing.
You heard me,
Not a darn thing!
I'm going to be right here on this couch
With my feet up
Chillin'
Because I'm tired.

I just know my man and my children
Are going to be looking for something to
Eat when they come in.
Shoot.
I'm hungry, too.
But I stopped at McDonald's on the way home.
I don't know what they're going to do,
And I'm not worried about it.
You know why?
Because I'm tired.

And you know what else?
I stink.
Now you know you stink when you can smell yourself.
And I do smell myself.
But right now I don't care about that either
Because I'm tired.

But, if I had the energy,
I'd change the linen on my bed,
Light some candles,
And run me a nice hot bubble bath.
Then I'd get into the tub and soak myself to prune
status,

Slide in between those crispy, clean sheets,
And, well,
It doesn't matter
Because I'm not going to do any of that.
I'm tired!

I really need to close my eyes while I'm sitting here, too,
Because looking around
Makes me see things that make me tired,
Like that bill lying on the table.
I need to pay it.
But I'm tired.
Or that glass beside the bill
Reminding me of the dishes
I left in the sink last night that need to be washed.
But I'm tired.
Even the table.
I need to dust it.
But I'm tired.

But putting things off
Knowing the work will be waiting for me
Is making me even more tired.
So I guess I'll get my tired self up
And cook dinner.

Our Routine Thing

Well, it's evening.
I'm about to fall into my nightly routine.
It starts with dinner. I'm not that original,
So it'll probably be some of the same old things

Like roast beef, fried chicken, pork chops, or a casserole
With rice, corn, macaroni and cheese, or mashed
potatoes,
Green beans or broccoli, and rolls.

Then my children will do their homework and
My husband will have the stereo on,
While I clean up the kitchen
And talk on the phone.

After that we'll all take a bath or shower,
Watch a little TV for about an hour,
Kiss and hug, say our prayers,
Turn off the lights, and say good-night.

That's Just Me

I'm different. I don't know why.
I'm not trying to be.
It's just who I am.
I've got my own personal program.

I go with the mood.
I don't dress to impress.
Some days every part of me is in place.
Other days I look a straight mess.

I don't need a lot of people
Around to be entertained.
I don't need to work out front
So that everybody can know my name.

I roll with the punches.
I turn with the tide.
I don't try to prove myself to anyone.
I know who I am inside.

But that's just me.
I've got to be free
To live according to what I believe
Without the weight of hypocrisy.

Mother, May I?

Neighborhood Mother

The minute you walked into her house
You knew that you were welcome.
She was the neighborhood mother.
She was maternal to us all.

If you had a problem,
She was there to listen.
If you were hungry,
She'd lead you to the kitchen.

If you were lost,
She'd help you find your way.
She was an angel.
She wouldn't let you fall.

She would give you anything.
All you had to do was ask
Because her heart believed
Everyone deserved a chance.

She'd slow you down if you moved too fast.
She'd say walk *after* you learn to crawl.
But, at the end of each accomplishment,
She'd make you feel ten feet tall.

She was the neighborhood mother.
She was living proof
That love seeds planted
Bring forth good fruit.

The Letter

Dear Mom,

This letter is a heart-felt thank you
For always coming to my rescue, and
For guiding me through stormy seasons
Despite my giving you every reason
To bail and, well,
Leave me in my hell to fail.

But you never gave up on me.
You always showed up.
It's forcing me to grow up,
To change my attitude,
And stop blaming everything on you.
You help me keep my chin up.

And now I want to live up
To all that I can be because of you.
When I get out of jail this time you'll see.

Love, Me

Let's Talk

I want to talk to you about something,
Although I'm not sure you'll understand.
After all, I'm a democrat,
You're a republican.
You voted for Bush, I voted for Kerry.
Against your wishes I got pregnant
Before deciding to marry.

I didn't go to college like you,
But my life is turning out okay.
My house is not in the suburbs like yours.
In the hood is where I stay.
I seem to have gone against
Everything you told me to do.
I hope I haven't been too much
Of a disappointment to you.

But, whether or not we're ever able
To share the same point of view,
What's important to me is knowing
I can share whatever kind of life I have with you,
That we can always communicate
In honesty and truth,
Heart to heart and soul to soul
About whatever I decide to do
Because you are my mother.
I count on you to be there 100 percent,
Guaranteed, and full-proof.

That's why I want to talk with you
About what's been on my mind.
Are you ready to hear what I'm about to say?
Can you handle my news this time?

Name Change

The other day my child
Came into my room to say,
"I've decided to change my name today."

I admit I was taken a little by surprise.
I even felt a tear try to fill up in one eye.
I've always encouraged her to speak her mind,
So, I asked why and she replied,

"It's a slave name
That doesn't adequately reflect who I am.
I want a name with meaning,
One that's African."

I had to think for a minute or so.
I had to find a gentle way to explain.
There was something she needed to know.
I wanted to keep it plain.

I said, "Baby, I know you're proud to be black.
And, believe me, Honey, there's nothing wrong with
that.
But, before you decide to do anything,
I want you to know how you got your name.

Back when I was carrying you
Being a pregnant teen was taboo.
But an older lady friend stepped in
And helped me prepare for you.

That allowed me to stay in school.
It was a beautiful thing to do.
So, I gave her name to you.
And she's African-*American* like *you.*

Your name already has personal meaning
For both me and you.
But, if you still want to change it, that's cool.
It's your name. Do what you want to do."

You

Long before she saw your face
A dream of you was in her heart of
A baby girl, healthy and smart,
A love connected child and friend,
If God would give her grace.

But several years of faithful trying
Left a sister sad with grief and
Bitter tears beyond belief,
The darkest echo to the sky
Until she was sick of crying.

So she turned her thoughts another way.
At last a chance for peace occurred.
No time to spend on dreams deferred.
She gave your name away
To a cat
That she found
And thought that that was that.
And then you came.

Sincerely Yours

Sleepless Night

Last night was another sleepless night
Spent tossing and turning until daylight.
I prayed for kids that were somehow forgotten,
Who are making mistakes because nobody taught
them.

I prayed for the child who was never told
That making wealth is oversold,
That kindness comes back seven fold,
That wisdom is the prize for growing old.

I prayed for the ones who never learned
How to give love or be loved in return,
That respect is given as it is earned,
That destructive ways defeat you until you turn.

I prayed for the youth who wasn't taught
That a person's honor can't be bought,
That God can't be found unless He's sought,
That victories won are battles fought.

I'll be praying for them again tonight.

Fellowship

Some people come to church
For a word from God,
While others come for the praise.
Me, I come for the fellowship.
I get strength from the various ways
That folks, unaware
Of how much they are giving,
Show how much they care
Just by being kind.
So, I anxiously await each time
We're together on one accord
With one mission in mind—
To serve the Lord
And brighten each other's day.

Quiet Time

At the end of the evening
When the sun has gone down,
And peace and quiet throughout
The house abounds,

That's when I can hear
A word from You.
That's when my ears
Are best in tune.

That's when we can
Relate and commune.
That's when I profess
My love to You.

In the evening hours
I steal away.
In the quiet time
Is when I pray
And plan with You
The upcoming day.

Need to Feed

That show is on again.
You know, the one about feeding hungry children.
I've seen it a million times.
Whenever I see it I cry
Because I feel so sorry for them.

At the end of the show I already know
I'll write a check to send.
It won't be much, but God will know
I wanted their pain to end.

Then I'll consider how blessed I am.
My soul will be glad for me
And sad for them.

The Cross

Two days before Easter on a Good Friday
A humble, sad-looking man walked by me
Carrying a wooden cross.
Silently down the street he walked.

My mind became fixed on contemplating
Thoughts of the Man he was imitating.
I thought of the cup that buried my sins,
And gave me the chance to live again,

And I began to praise Him.